DEFILED

or

The Convenience of a Short-Haired Dog

A Play by
Lee Kalcheim

A Samuel French Acting Edition

New York Hollywood London Toronto
SAMUELFRENCH.COM

Copyright © 2000, 2002 by Lee Kalcheim

ALL RIGHTS RESERVED

CAUTION: Professionals and amateurs are hereby warned that *DEFILED* is subject to a Licensing Fee. It is fully protected under the copyright laws of the United States of America, the British Commonwealth, including Canada, and all other countries of the Copyright Union. All rights, including professional, amateur, motion picture, recitation, lecturing, public reading, radio broadcasting, television and the rights of translation into foreign languages are strictly reserved. In its present form the play is dedicated to the reading public only.

The amateur live stage performance rights to *DEFILED* are controlled exclusively by Samuel French, Inc., and licensing arrangements and performance licenses must be secured well in advance of presentation. PLEASE NOTE that amateur Licensing Fees are set upon application in accordance with your producing circumstances. When applying for a licensing quotation and a performance license please give us the number of performances intended, dates of production, your seating capacity and admission fee. Licensing Fees are payable one week before the opening performance of the play to Samuel French, Inc., at 45 W. 25th Street, New York, NY 10010.

Licensing Fee of the required amount must be paid whether the play is presented for charity or gain and whether or not admission is charged.

Stock licensing fees quoted upon application to Samuel French, Inc.

For all other rights than those stipulated above, apply to: Barbara Hogenson Agency, 165 West End Ave., Ste 19C, New York, NY 10023.

Particular emphasis is laid on the question of amateur or professional readings, permission and terms for which must be secured in writing from Samuel French, Inc.

Copying from this book in whole or in part is strictly forbidden by law, and the right of performance is not transferable.

Whenever the play is produced the following notice must appear on all programs, printing and advertising for the play: "Produced by special arrangement with Samuel French, Inc."

Due authorship credit must be given on all programs, printing and advertising for the play.

ISBN 978-0-573-62835-1

No one shall commit or authorize any act or omission by which the copyright of, or the right to copyright, this play may be impaired.

No one shall make any changes in this play for the purpose of production.

Publication of this play does not imply availability for performance. Both amateurs and professionals considering a production are strongly advised in their own interests to apply to Samuel French, Inc., for written permission before starting rehearsals, advertising, or booking a theatre.

No part of this book may be reproduced, stored in a retrieval system, or transmitted in any form, by any means, now known or yet to be invented, including mechanical, electronic, photocopying, recording, videotaping, or otherwise, without the prior written permission of the publisher.

MUSIC USE NOTE

Licensees are solely responsible for obtaining formal written permission from copyright owners to use copyrighted music in the performance of this play and are strongly cautioned to do so. If no such permission is obtained by the licensee, then the licensee must use only original music that the licensee owns and controls. Licensees are solely responsible and liable for all music clearances and shall indemnify the copyright owners of the play and their licensing agent, Samuel French, Inc., against any costs, expenses, losses and liabilities arising from the use of music by licensees.

IMPORTANT BILLING AND CREDIT REQUIREMENTS

All producers of *DEFILED* *must* give credit to the Author of the Play in all programs distributed in connection with performances of the Play, and in all instances in which the title of the Play appears for the purposes of advertising, publicizing or otherwise exploiting the Play and/or a production. The name of the Author *must* appear on a separate line on which no other name appears, immediately following the title and *must* appear in size of type not less than fifty percent of the size of the title type. In addition, credits for the original producers of the Play must appear on the title page of all programs distributed in connection with performances of the Play. Credits must substantially be as follows:

DEFILED
or
The Convenience of a Short-haired Dog

A PLAY BY
Lee Kalcheim

Originally Produced by Geffen Playhouse
Gilbert Cates, Producing Director
Lou Moore, Managing Director
Los Angeles 2000

DEFILED

by
Lee Kalhein

premiered in Los Angeles on May 31, 2000 at the

Geffen Playhouse

Gilbert Gates, *Producing Director*
Lou Moore, *Managing Director*
Randall Arney, *Artistic Director*
Amy Levinson, *Literary Manager*

Cast:

HARRY MENDELSSOHN	Jason Alexander
BRIAN DICKEY	Peter Falk
MELINDA	Nancy Mette
SENTANA	David Speilberg
Understudy	Fred Sanders
Director	Barnet Kellman
Set Designer	D. Martyn Bookwalter
Costume Designer	Tom McKinley
Lightening Designer	Daniel Ioanzzi
Sound	John Gottlieb
Production Stage Manager	Elsbeth M. Collins

THE CHARACTERS

HARRY MENDELSSOHN
BRIAN DICKEY

<u>OFF-STAGE VOICES:</u>
MELINDA
SENTANA

THE SETTING

The main room of a large metropolitan library

THE TIME
Late Twentieth Century

(The play should be performed without intermission.)

FOR JULIA

(SCENE: The main room of a large metropolitan library. A grand old room in a grand old building. Time: 1990's. Outside we can hear the sounds of police sirens, helicopters, muffled crowd activity.)

In the large main room, HARRY MENDELSSOHN, a man whose age lurks just on either side of forty, is taping to a column many sticks of dynamite taped together with other electronic equipment--a bomb. We see other packets of dynamite are taped to other columns in the room.

HARRY inspects the bomb, moves over to the check out desk, picks up a remote control device. He holds it out in a mock drill of setting off bomb. Takes a deep breath and puts it in his shirt pocket. Misses the pocket. The remote drops on the floor. He jumps back throwing his hands up as if to protect himself from the bomb blast. Nothing. He sighs a huge sigh. He bends over and picks up remote. Now, carefully puts it in his pocket.

The phone rings. He moves to desk, picks up phone and takes it off the hook.

Then, from outside the building we hear a voice on an electronic megaphone. It is DETECTIVE BRIAN DICKEY.)

BRIAN. *(O.S.)* Harry! Mr. Mendelssohn. This is Detective Dickey. I just want to talk to you. Could you put the phone back on the hook so we could talk? *(HARRY hesitates.)* Mr. Mendelssohn if I could just talk to you for a minute. If you'd just ...

(HARRY sighs, moves to phone.)

HARRY. Oh for God's sake ....

(HARRY moves to the phone and puts it back on the hook.)

BRIAN. *(O.S.)* ... put the phone back on the hook so I could ask you a few things, I think ....What? OK.

(Phone rings. HARRY picks it up.)

HARRY. Hello. Look, I don't want to talk to you. I want you to take the trucks away. You know what I want. There's nothing to talk about. No! I've seen movies. I've seen lots of movies. You want to negotiate. You'll come in here and negotiate me out of this. No! No negotiation!! *(He hangs up. He starts upstage. Phone rings again. He returns to the phone.)* I told you ... what? What long distance company am I using? I have no idea. I'm not interested. I don't care how much I can save on MCI, I'm not interested. This is not a good time to ....

(HARRY hangs up. Remembers, takes it off the hook. He puts down the remote on the desk. He begins straightening up his desk. He returns a book to the upstage shelves. The front door opens. He turns quickly, grabbing the bomb remote from the desk.
We see BRIAN DICKEY, Detective, pushing sixty. Ruddy Irish face. Bit overweight.)

BRIAN. Hold it. Hold it. Don't do anything stupid. I'm unarmed. Look.

(BRIAN opens coat. Shows.)

HARRY. How did you get in here?
BRIAN. You didn't lock the door.
HARRY. *(HARRY shakes his head at his own mistake. Then, as BRIAN takes a step forward, he points the remote.)* Don't come in here. I'll blow this place!
BRIAN. I'm not armed.
HARRY. Stay back. I'll set this off.
BRIAN. I'm here to talk.
HARRY. I don't want talk. I want action. I'm gonna do it!

DEFILED 9

BRIAN. Don't do it.
HARRY. I'm going to do it!
BRIAN. Don't.
HARRY. I'm going to do it.
BRIAN. Don't. Please don't.
HARRY. Please? Who are you. Are you with SOLC?
BRIAN. SOLC?
HARRY. Save Our Libraries Committee.
BRIAN. No. I'm Detective Dickey.
HARRY. A cop.
BRIAN. Yes, but I like libraries.
HARRY. You're just saying that.
BRIAN. No I'm not just saying that.
HARRY. What's the last book you took out of the library?
BRIAN. I don't remember.
HARRY. You don't remember? How long ago was it?
BRIAN. I don't know. Forty, fifty years.
HARRY. The last time you were in a library was fifty years ago?
BRIAN. Maybe more.
HARRY. What the hell are you doing here now?
BRIAN. I'm trying to stop you from blowing it up.
HARRY. You?? Why do you care? You wouldn't miss it.
BRIAN. You're probably right. But it's my job.
HARRY. What's your job? Saving libraries. They could at least have picked a guy who used one occasionally.
BRIAN. That's not my job.
HARRY. What?
BRIAN. Saving libraries. My job is saving lives. I'm a police detective.
HARRY. When's the last time you saved a life?
BRIAN. Day before yesterday.
HARRY. Really? Who?
BRIAN. Can we talk about your life? Can we talk about what's going on here?
HARRY. Who did you save?
BRIAN. It doesn't *matter*.

HARRY. It matters to me.

BRIAN. Hector Rodriguez.

HARRY. Who's he?

BRIAN. He is a painter. An artist. He got rejected at the Art Academy.

HARRY. Like Hitler.

BRIAN. What?

HARRY. If they'd accepted Hitler into art school, millions of people's lives would have been saved. So *shortsighted*!!!!

BRIAN. Right. Well, he got rejected and wanted to kill himself. Tried to jump off the Warneke Expressway Bridge into rush hour traffic. It would have been a mess. I talked him down.

HARRY. What did you say?

BRIAN. I don't remember. But I must have said the right thing.

HARRY. You know what I would have said?

BRIAN. No.

HARRY. "If you can't take rejection, you shouldn't be an artist!"

BRIAN. I didn't say that.

HARRY. You should have. People facing suicide need a dose of reality. My sister is suicidal. I sometimes just say to her; "Life *is* awful. But we're not all trying to kill ourselves. If everyone who was depressed tried to kill themselves the streets would be clogged with bodies."

BRIAN. I see.

HARRY. She's still around.

BRIAN. Good, look ...

HARRY. Don't move. This thing'll blow us both up. The whole building.

BRIAN. Y'know ... you're timing really isn't good with this thing.

HARRY. I beg your pardon?

BRIAN. I mean with nuts all over the world who're blowin' things up, I don't think it's gonna help your cause going about it this way.

HARRY. There is no one in the building but me. I'm not a terrorist. I'm a fatalist!

BRIAN. Ah hah.

HARRY. Terrorists are fanatics. They don't care about human consequences. I'm doing this for humanity.

BRIAN. They probably say the same thing.

HARRY. It's not! No matter what I do, this building will be gone. In ten years. Gone. The real estate is too valuable for a library. I'm ... I'm trying to save it.

BRIAN. Okay.

HARRY. I'm not a thug. I'm not a callous criminal. I want to save this place.

BRIAN. Good. Good. Look, I wanna find a way to help you out. Okay? Find a way out of this mess, okay?

HARRY. I'm not negotiating.

BRIAN. Absolutely not! You have very strong feelings about what you want and it's really not my place to change your mind. I mean I don't know anything about this. I just ... I'm just trying to work this thing out so you can get what you want ... and we can all go home. *(They just both stand a moment.)* So ... I'm gonna come in okay? You've got that thing so I can't do anything, so I'm gonna come in. *(Comes in to the top level. HARRY crosses warily to the left of his desk. BRIAN looks around.)* It's a real nice library here. Real nice. *(Turns to HARRY.)* So ...Well, ... I don't really know very much about this whole mess. I've been hearing from this guy Stockerfield. He's some big wig at uh ...

HARRY. He's the executive head of the Consolidated Libraries.

BRIAN. Okay. Well ... he's ... he's very upset. He doesn't want you to blow up his library.

HARRY. HIS library? HIS. This library was built by Cyrus Latham Wells in 1879 when Stockerfield's Grandfather was driving a milk wagon. This was one of the great pieces of Architecture of its time. It still is.

BRIAN. Yes. It is a very ... very grand building. I agree.

HARRY. It belongs to the public. To the people. Not to Stockerfield.

BRIAN. Uh huh. Well, look I figured I really ought to hear from *you* what's going on here. I mean if you want to blow this place up, a nice place like this, you must be pretty upset. You must have a pretty good reason. Stockerfield ... he doesn't *know* the reason. He just thinks you went off the deep end or something, but I gotta at least give you the benefit of the doubt and let you tell me what the problem is to see ... y'know if we can come to some kind of understanding.

HARRY. I told you NO NEG-

BRIAN. I'm not gonna do that. I told you. I'm here to find out from you ... right from you why you want to blow up this really fine building. I mean I'm curious. Okay? You want some coffee? *(He pulls thermos out of his coat pocket. HARRY reacts.)* It's just a thermos. Coffee. *(BRIAN moves to the desk. Opens thermos and pours some.)* You want some coffee?

HARRY. It's drugged.

BRIAN. My wife made it this morning. She makes pretty good coffee.

HARRY. It's drugged.

BRIAN. Maybe that's why it's so good. *(Takes a sip.)* You sure? *(HARRY nods.)* Remember when you could only get one kind of coffee. Coffee. Now it's got flavors. Weird flavors. My son drinks this stuff made with grain. Caffix. Has no coffee in it at all. *(He stops, looks around.)* Jesus, this really is quite a building.

HARRY. Wells designed it when he was thirty-two. It was only his second building. His last was the state capitol.

BRIAN. Oh yeah? That's some building too. He did 'em both?

HARRY. Forty years apart. This one's better. Did it himself. Everybody and their cousins had something to say about the capitol. Politicians make messes. This was his masterpiece. *(HARRY crosses downstage of his desk.)* You know you can stand at the far end there and whisper and be heard anywhere in the room.

BRIAN. Is that good for a library?

HARRY. They use it sometimes for concerts.

BRIAN. Ah. Well. Yeah. That's okay. Anyhow, I'll just leave the coffee here. *(BRIAN picks up the thermos, crosses left and puts it down on Harry's desk. HARRY checks it for microphones.)* You want some. You take it. It's nice and hot. Okay? So— What's this all about?

DEFILED 13

HARRY. What did Stockerfield tell you?

BRIAN. Oh he's just ranting and raving. I couldn't get much outta him.

HARRY. He show you my note?

BRIAN. Oh. Oh yeah. *(He pulls note out of his pocket and reads.)* "Since you have seen fit to ignore my request that the card files remain, I will destroy the entire library."

HARRY. You understand?

BRIAN. What?

HARRY. What I want?

BRIAN. You want to keep the card files here.

HARRY. Yes.

BRIAN. Uh huh. *(He moves to and indicates the card files.)* These them?

HARRY. Yes.

BRIAN. I remember these. When I was a kid I used 'em a couple of times on Library Day. Those days they would take us to the library and show us how the place worked. We'd take out a book. *(He opens a drawer.)* All the books are listed in here.

HARRY. Yes.

BRIAN. I remember the book I took out. It was a Hardy Boys book. The Hardy Boys go ... somewhere.

HARRY. Great.

BRIAN. Good book. I'm not much of a reader.

HARRY. Really.

BRIAN. You must be.

HARRY. I read quite a bit.

BRIAN. All of these.

HARRY. Not nearly.

BRIAN. Take a while I'll bet. So--what's so important about keeping these things? I mean you wanna blow this place up. Blow yourself up for --a couple of file cabinets? What's the deal?

HARRY. The "deal" is; There're going to take them out and destroy them and replace them completely with those computers."

BRIAN. Uh huh. Well that's happenin' all over. We got 'em. And ... I've got one at home so my grandson can use it. You don't like 'em huh?

HARRY. They have their place.

BRIAN. And this isn't it, right?

HARRY. You could say that.

BRIAN. Uh huh, well ...

HARRY. So I asked. I pleaded with Stockerfield not to throw the files away. I said we could have the computers and the card files. He refused. Finally I just called him a shortsighted ignorant bastard and the son of a bitch fired me. After fifteen years. Just like that. That's when I got the idea.

BRIAN. To blow up the library.

HARRY. Yes.

BRIAN. Because you were fired.

HARRY. NO! Because he wouldn't keep the files. Because he didn't understand their value. It's computers or nothing. And it will soon all be ... nothing. I don't want to hurt anyone. But Stockerfield is out there with trucks to take away these files and he's not going to get them. He'll never get them! I'll die before he gets them!

BRIAN. Fine. Good. I'm learnin' something. See, it's important we talk. I'm learning something. Oh, can I put this phone back on in case they want to get me?

HARRY. Well ....

BRIAN. In case there's an emergency ... y'know.

HARRY. You would leave here for *another* emergency?

BRIAN. No. *(Laughs.)* Sorry. No. I'm not going anywhere. It's just a precaution. If you change your mind, I'll take it off.

(BRIAN moves to phone and replaces receiver.)

HARRY. You think this is frivolous, right?

BRIAN. Frivolous?

HARRY. You think this is a joke. A man is willing to blow up an entire library—kill himself—just to prevent them from throwing out their card files!

BRIAN. I don't think it's a j—

HARRY. It's not a joke.

DEFILED 15

(HARRY yanks the phone off the hook.)

BRIAN. I don't think it's a joke. You don't look like a guy who would joke. You look like a very intelligent guy. A very serious guy.

HARRY. You think I'm crazy.

BRIAN. I don't think you're crazy. Stockerfield. He thinks you're crazy. That's why I came in here. I don't think so. I think … this is too … this is … this is kind of your … I think this is urgent for you. Very urgent. This is something I think you have a very good reason for … to want to blow up this beautiful place. I think you love this place. You worked here … fifteen years, right. And I think you're very upset. I can see that. I can feel that. I know that.

HARRY. You don't know anything. You'd say all this to me if I was a raving lunatic holding a bunch of hostages at a Seven-Eleven.

BRIAN. No I wouldn't.

HARRY. You're negotiating! I told you NO NEGOTIATING!

BRIAN. I'm trying to find out what the hell is so important about a bunch of filing cabinets?? If you can tell me what is so important, maybe I can help you here. *(HARRY starts to laugh.)* I said something funny?

HARRY. No. I just … I'm amused by this.

BRIAN. Uh huh. What's amusing?

HARRY. You wouldn't understand.

BRIAN. Hey, I don't have a graduate degree in amusement, but I understand quite a few things.

HARRY. Okay.

BRIAN. You're wondering why they sent me in to talk to you. You want to talk to someone who understands you, right? Who understands why these … these files are important. Someone like Stockerfield. Stockerfield … your boss … who understands all this is outside jumping up and down like a raving lunatic. If he comes in here he's gonna set that bomb off just by ….

HARRY. I don't want to talk to him.

BRIAN. I mean he understands what ….

HARRY. He has no idea! I don't want. Forget it! You don't understand what's amusing. You don't understand why I want the files .

You don't understand. It's all right.

BRIAN. No it's not all right. My job is to understand what you want.

HARRY. Okay.

BRIAN. I'm supposed to be good at that. You know my wife says I don't understand her, but ... you know she's ... Italian. What can I say. She's a different person every day of the week. You look like the kind of guy. You get up every morning. You're the same guy.

HARRY. Uh huh.

BRIAN. You worked here fifteen years. You love books. You married?

HARRY. You don't know?

BRIAN. They don't tell me everything. I pull up in a car. They say ... he's in there. He's gonna blow the place up. They give me your note. And I hear you worked here fifteen years. And you never gave anyone any trouble. You sound fine. For a guy who wants to blow up a building. So I don't know very much at all. You married?

HARRY. No.

BRIAN. You gay?

HARRY. No. All unmarried men have to be gay?

BRIAN. No.

HARRY. If I was gay, they'd bring in the gay expert?

BRIAN. No. I just ... I don't know. It ... I got a son who may be gay.

HARRY. May be?

BRIAN. Well ... we don't know yet. He doesn't date. But ...WE can talk about this some other time.... My Chief is outside and I figure he's looking at his watch ... y'know.... We can get together after this is over and talk about life.

HARRY. You care if your son is gay?

BRIAN. Yeah. No. I don't know. I got two other sons. One can be gay, that's okay. *(HARRY looks at him doubtfully.)* One writes for advertising. Big company. Very big. In Los Angeles. We never see him. the other one played pro ball. Minor leagues. Double A. Tough going. He's just ... divorced. He's livin' with us for awhile. Lookin' for work. It's hard on my wife, but y'know that's what families are for. Your folks alive?

HARRY. No.

BRIAN. Uh huh. Sisters? Brothers?

HARRY. Sister. Lives in St. Louis. Don't call her. She's very depressed. If you call her she'll get you depressed. You call her she just sucks you into her life. Her problems. So if you have any idea that her talking to me would be helpful in this matter, you couldn't be more wrong.

BRIAN. Fine.

HARRY. I mean if you're in a hurry, she's not the one to call.

BRIAN. I'm not in a hurry.

HARRY. You said your chief was looking at his watch.

BRIAN. He's the chief. He wants to resolve this quickly. My job is to resolve this peacefully. Nobody hurt. I'm in no hurry.

(They stand a second. BRIAN waiting for HARRY. HARRY unsure ... then ...)

HARRY. Can ... can I have some coffee?

BRIAN. Absolutely. *(He picks up thermos to pour as HARRY brings out a cup and takes some.)* It's got sugar in it. Okay?

HARRY. I like sugar.

BRIAN. I tried getting off of sugar. Y'know, to lose a little of this. *(Tummy.)* But that artificial stuff is ... awful. You'd think with all the money these guys have they could come up with something artificial that's real.

HARRY. Fortunately they can't.

BRIAN. What?

HARRY. There are few things left that can't be duplicated. I rather admire sugar for being so difficult.

BRIAN. Okay.

HARRY. Once something can be duplicated, it loses its value. It is no longer ... unique. But of course the word "unique" has lost its value. Because everyday I hear a person say, "that something or other is very unique." How can something be very unique? Unique is an absolute!

BRIAN. Okay.

HARRY. When the food geniuses invented instant coffee they thought, "no one will ever brew coffee again." They were wrong. There is hope. *(He sips coffee.)* Nice coffee. My compliments to your wife.

BRIAN. Yeah. She's ... she makes good coffee. Good everything. Great cook.

HARRY. Different person everyday but always a great cook.

BRIAN. Yeah. She can ... y'know we can have a knock down drag out fight ... and then she can run off to the kitchen and make something incredible. What ever it is that makes her cook good ... just you know ... is not affected by how she feels. Not like me. I have a terrible day. I can't do anything.

HARRY. What is it that you do?

BRIAN. Huh?

HARRY. What do you do that a terrible day could affect?

BRIAN. Oh ... nothing much . I ... fish. That's pretty much all I do. Trout. Make my own flies. It's very ... delicate work. I don't look delicate but I can do that. And if I have a bad day, I can't do it. I just sit and drink and watch TV. She can cook. So, you never got married.

HARRY. No. I ... No.

BRIAN. You what? You had a girlfriend?

HARRY. You know that.

BRIAN. No. No I don't. I'm just guessing. Wondering. You had a girlfriend.

HARRY. I was engaged. Many years ago. I was in college.

BRIAN. Where?

HARRY. Here. At the university.

BRIAN. Uh huh. What happened?

HARRY. She broke it off.

BRIAN. Uh huh. That happens. And ...?

HARRY. And, we didn't get married. That's all.

BRIAN. Where is she now?

HARRY. She lives in a house in the suburbs. She's married and lives in one of those ... homes.

BRIAN. You ... still keep in touch?

HARRY. *(Crosses to stage right computer table.)* She sends me a

Christmas card. I don't open it. I opened one years ago. It had one of those detailed Xeroxed letters about every little things she and her hubby had done the whole year. Depressing.

BRIAN. So you haven't talked to her in ...

(HARRY slams his cup down onto the table and walks briskly upstage into the stacks.)

HARRY. I don't want to talk about this!

BRIAN. Fine. Fine. So, ... there's nobody else?

HARRY. No.

BRIAN. Uh huh. OK. So, you have this sister. And that's it. Some friends, right?

HARRY. Not really. I'm the classic "loner". *(HARRY peers around the right column. Ironically:)* He was a "loner" they said after he murdered seventy five people at the mall.

BRIAN. You don't seem like a "loner." You work here. You must ... talk to hundreds of people a day. It's a very ... very social kind of job. Loners don't do that.

HARRY. Well I guess I'm a sociable loner.

BRIAN. I don't think you're a loner.

HARRY. Does it matter?

BRIAN. What?

HARRY. Does it matter what I am????

BRIAN. No, I ...

HARRY. What the hells' the difference what I am. Whether I'm married. Whether I'm straight or gay or Russian or Greek, or Jewish or gentile or Muslim or diabetic or what? I want those trucks outside to go away. That's who I am. That's all that matters. I want them to go away and leave these files here. That's all that matters.

BRIAN. You're right. That's all that matters.

HARRY. Thank you. You're so considerate.

BRIAN Hey, I'm trying to help.

HARRY. You're trying to save the building.

BRIAN. I'm trying to help.

HARRY. The library is a valuable piece of property. It's an eco-

nomic issue.
    BRIAN. No, I just don't want you to die for something dumb.
    HARRY. I beg your pardon.
    BRIAN. I meant ....
    HARRY. No that's what you meant.
    BRIAN. I'm sorry.
    HARRY. Don't be sorry. That's what you meant.
    BRIAN. No I meant.

(HARRY crosses downstage with purpose.)

    HARRY. That's what you meant and it's fine. It's FINE! You think this cause is dumb. That's fine. It's perfect. You say you understand. You don't understand. And that's fine. Because as soon as I make you understand. As soon as I get you to understand. You will be on my side. *(BRIAN, upset by his gaff, just throws up his hands. HARRY moves to files.)* Come here.
    BRIAN. Huh?
    HARRY. Come here. I want to show you something. *(BRIAN starts toward him.)* Don't do anything stupid. If I push this button, neither of us will be a very pretty sight. *(HARRY beckons him to come and moves to the card file, BRIAN follows.)* You ever used one of these?
    BRIAN. Sure ... the ....
    HARRY. Oh, right the Hardy Boys. Find it.
    BRIAN. What?
    HARRY. Find the Hardy Boys book you read.
    BRIAN. I don't even remember the title.
    HARRY. You can do it. Try. For me.

(BRIAN gives him a look, smiles and turns to the file.)

    BRIAN. Hardy boys. "H." *(Looks for H file. Finds opens it. Looks through the cards)* Hardy Boys. Hardy Boys. Jeeze there are a lot.... Hey. Here it is. "The Hardy Boys Go West." That was it. *(Pulls out card.)* "The Hardy Boys Go West."

DEFILED 21

HARRY. You found it.
BRIAN. Yeah.
HARRY. Took you about ten seconds. Not bad. *(HARRY starts toward computer table.)* Think you could do it as fast on a computer?
BRIAN. I don't know.
HARRY. Try it.

(BRIAN goes to the computer and sits. HARRY stand behind him, slightly stage right.)

BRIAN. Okay, what do I do?
HARRY. *(Turns it on.)* Hit "return." *(BRIAN does this.)* Okay, now find "The Hardy Boys."
BRIAN. How?
HARRY. Well, start by typing in "T" for title. Then type in the title.
BRIAN. I don't type so well.
HARRY. Do your best.
BRIAN. *(Types.)* H-A-R-D-Y B-O-Y-S. *(Looks at screen.)* Oh look, it says "You searched for this title—Hardy Boys— 2 titles found with fourteen entries." What's an entry?
HARRY. Never mind. Hit 1.
BRIAN. *(Hits key, then reads:)* "Title: The Hidden Harbor Mystery" That's not it. We're looking for "The Hardy Boys Go West." Now what?
HARRY. You have to go back to the main menu. But don't bother. It's taken you about a minute already to find the wrong title. You'll have to keep going down the list until you find the right one. It only took you ten seconds in the catalogue. I had a bunch of second graders in here the other day. Seven-year-olds. They zip through the cards.
BRIAN. Well they can learn to use the computer. Kids are good at that. My grandson's a whiz.
HARRY. At what? Playing games. Ugly monsters destroying uglier monsters.
BRIAN. No, he's got this whole encyclopedia. Comes up on the

screen. With pictures that talk. It's fantastic.

HARRY. It's a cartoon encyclopedia. Three lines of information and a dinosaur that roars. No real content.

BRIAN. He likes it.

HARRY. It's entertainment. *(HARRY moves DSL of desk. He indicates the card file.)* But is it helpful? Is he learning anything? These cards teach. And they are efficient. This is a brilliant system.

BRIAN. They can always make improvements. *(BRIAN stands and crosses left toward HARRY.)* I mean when I was a kid we only had radio. Now we have TV.

HARRY. And the world's a better place.

BRIAN. I don't know about that but ....

HARRY. And people read fewer books.

BRIAN. No, actually I saw an article where it says they read more.

HARRY. How-to-books by TV stars.

BRIAN. Hey, they're reading books. You should be happy. Keep your job.

HARRY. I already lost my job.

BRIAN. Well, it's not the computer's fault, right?

HARRY. It will be. Librarians will lose their jobs. But that is not what this is about. This is about the grandeur of man. The loss of the grandeur of man.

BRIAN. Yeah, well ....

HARRY. Since the dawn of civilization, man has been keeping records. Inventories of their experiences. On tooth necklaces. On message sticks and tattoos. On quipus: knotted pieces of rope that have been found as distant from each other as China and Peru. And once man learned to write there was an explosion of record keeping. In the Fourth Century BC, in Mesopotamia, men carved words in clay tablets ... "cuneiform" and then *filed* them in large wicker baskets. In Alexandria, *(HARRY moves upstage to top level, reveling in his library. BRIAN comes to the right of Harry's desk.)* the Greeks built a great library to store papyrus rolls. And in Rome, Julius Caesar was so jealous of it he planned to build a great state library of his own, but was assassinated before he could realize his ambitions. The first mar-

tyr to the cause. And then came 1448. Do you know what happened in 1448?
BRIAN. Christopher Columbus ....

(HARRY moves downstage to the right of BRIAN.)

HARRY. Was born three years later. But Johan Guttenberg. Very much alive. Invented movable type.
BRIAN. What?

(HARRY paces stage right to the right of the computer table.)

HARRY. The printing press! And changed the world. More people wrote. More people read. And the English, having a lousy climate, read more. So for all those books, in 1604, Sir Thomas Bodely creates a brilliant catalogue for the Royal Library. But of course, the more people read, the more people in power felt reading was dangerous. So cataloguing is invented, followed immediately by ... you guessed it ... censorship! The French Revolutionary government catalogued their banned books by listing them on small pieces of paper tied together with string and invented "the card file." There was refinement after refinement. A hundred years later, an American, Melville Dewey, refines the refiners. He invents the Dewey decimal system. The brilliant filing system we still use today. Even in the computers. From Babylonia in 4000 BC to today, man has perfected the system. Trained librarians to execute it. To list and cross reference each book, and guide each and every reader to the book he needs. The system works. It is fast. It is personal. It is perfect. Why change it just to change?
BRIAN. Well maybe there's just too many books today. I mean too many to put in those drawers there. I mean that's what happened with us. We were gettin' so many calls on 911, they had to computerize the system. I mean you gotta be realistic. You gotta be practical.
HARRY. You sound like my father. He was a practical man. He ran a hardware store. What could be more practical than hardware. I loved to go down to the store. I didn't see it the way he did. Rows and rows and rows of useful things. I saw it as this great cacophony of

stuff! Tools. Wonderful tools. Some that had not changed shape or function since the Assyrians. All piled high in his narrow store. He saw the use of these tools as practical. I saw it as cosmic.! *(BRIAN nods, skeptically.)* Fine. That's fine. But then, ... when I was nine, my father said he was going to buy me a dog. "What kind of dog do you want?," he asked. "A collie," I said. "Just like Lassie. A collie." He shook his head...."Nnnnno. Collies are too big. Knock over things. Hair's too long. They shed. Not convenient. I'm gonna get you a small short- haired dog. That barks at strangers. Much better." And that's what he got me. This small, short-haired ... convenient dog. Not the dog I could wrestle with and fold myself into his long hair. Not the dog I could ride and wrestle with and play with. He got me a convenient dog. I never forgave him.

BRIAN. So now you have a collie?

HARRY. Yes! In my small apartment. And it is not convenient. For either of us. But I have it.

BRIAN. Well good. You got what you wanted.

HARRY. Not when I wanted it.

BRIAN. Hey I always wanted a sports car. I'm never gonna get it. I don't make that kind of money.

HARRY. You should get it.

BRIAN. No. It's a crime to pay forty thousand dollars for a car. It's just a car.

HARRY. Get a used one.

BRIAN. It's not that important. I'm too old now . I couldn't get into one of 'em. So.

HARRY. Get one anyhow.

BRIAN. No, I don't think so.

HARRY. It's not practical. It's not convenient.

BRIAN. It's not practical. It's not convenient and it's not even what I want anymore. You see when you get older, what you want changes. It's a nice thing actually. You gotta' recognize it when it happens. Cars are important when you're young. I'm lookin' at retirement in a couple of years. I'm lookin' maybe to go off to Ireland, where my grandfather came from. Go back to the upper reaches of the Liffey River and fish. In God's green country. That's what I want now. That and ... to stay alive. My wife's always worried that something's gonna happen to me, cause I'm gettin' to retirement. She thinks I oughta be doing safer work at my age. It's no picnic being married to a cop. Lyin' to your wife and kids. Wonderin' if some nut's gonna .... So. I'd like to go and fish in the Liffey.... Isn't there some place you'd like to go?

HARRY. Sure. I'd like to go to Paris. Or to Italy, where I was supposed to go with my girlfriend, but we ... I went alone and it was wonderful. But ....

BRIAN. So hey. Go back. That's somethin' to want. That's somethin' you can have. As a matter of fact, that is something I can help you get. Right now. You give this all up ... Harry ... I'm gonna tell you right now, I will get you a free ticket *to Paris* or Italy. Take a friend. That's something, huh?

HARRY. You're negotiating.

BRIAN. Yes. Yes I am. but don't take offense. My wife say I do it in my sleep.

(Seeing Brian's tactic, HARRY crosses away to stage left of his desk.)

HARRY. I'm not interested.

BRIAN. Harry, think about it. Tomorrow you could be in Italy.

HARRY. And you know where these file cards would be? They'll be dumped into a landfill somewhere, and covered over to form the "bedrock" of yet another interminable shopping mall.

BRIAN. Harry, you can't stop it. It's progress. If it's gonna happen, it's gonna happen. It may not be for the best. You may be right. But they'll find that out and then maybe they'll bring the files back and call you up and say "Harry, you were right. We're sorry." But you can't force them to agree with you. They gotta find out for themselves.

HARRY. It'll be too late. The cards will be gone!

BRIAN. So you'll make new cards!

(HARRY is getting agitated. He crosses to SR of the computer table.)

HARRY. NO!! That's the point. They are making new cards

now —entries in the database, and they are no good! They're dumbed down versions of what cards used to be. Even when the library of congress made cards for our huge library system, they culled cards from the great libraries. And made great cards. Now in a windowless room in mid America, tepid ... ghosts of these cards are abridged, often misspelled, and entered into the data base by people who have no idea what they're copying. It's like trying to find a book at Barnes and Nobel from a salesclerk who never heard of your book, never heard of your author and probably doesn't read. *(He walks to the file, opens, pulls out card.)* These cards are unique. The great librarians of the great libraries made entries by hand on each card. Made specific, personal analyses of each book. When you found a card say for ... Swift's "A Modest Proposal" ....

BRIAN. What?

HARRY. "A Modest Proposal." It was a pamphlet that Jonathan Swift wrote in 1729, during a famine in Ireland. In it he proposed that the children of the poor be sold as food for the tables of the wealthy.

BRIAN. You're kidding!

HARRY. You can read it yourself. I'll find it for you.

(HARRY heads off right into the stacks, looking at the card.)

BRIAN. People went along with this idea?

HARRY. It was ... a joke. To point out to the British government how inept their policies were in dealing with the food shortage. While Parliament dithered, and people died, Swift wrote his modest proposal.

(HARRY returns carrying a small leather-bound book. He crosses to the right of BRIAN.)

BRIAN. Did they get it?

HARRY. What?

BRIAN. The joke.

HARRY. Barely. Look ... my point is ... that a great librarian will explain ... on a card ... to people just like you, just how important such a piece of literature is. Its historical significance. Its influence on other books. Encouraging you to seek those other books. When these cards become landfill, or wallboard, or Wall Street confetti ... all that will be left are the sterile cards in the data base ... that lead you without enthusiasm, nakedly to your book.

BRIAN. Wait a minute, the whole thing about computers is that they're fast. And you can cram a lot of information into them. So why can't they take library cards from all these guys and put 'em all into their card?

HARRY. It's not practical. It's not convenient. We watch the news today in sound bites. We want sound bite library cards.

BRIAN. Okay, so the computers aren't so great. They still get you to the books. That's what they're for.

HARRY. But they don't send you to the book. Or if they send you to the book, it's not the right book. Or not the best book! Look ... say I'm a student—I'm writing a paper for school ... on ... political satire. Ok? I go to the computer . *(He does, laying the remote down.)* I type in "Political Satire" *(He types it in, then picks up the remote.)* It says "You searched for the subject; Political Satire. 79 subjects found with 229 entries. Subjects 1 to 8 are:" *(He now goes down the list.)* "1. Political Satire, 17 entries; 2. Political Satire, American, 15 entries; 3. Political Satire, American Exhibitions, 1 entry; 4. Political Satire, American History 19th Century, 1 entry." It goes on.... Lets hit number one just for kicks. *(Hits 1.)* Under the first subject heading for political satire we have: "1. The Big Red Joke Book, 2. Burtos Consejos Para Govermantes, 3. Les Hommes Politiques ont de l'humour, 4. Die Karakatur al Medium in der politischen Bildu, 5. Liberte, Egalatie, Hilarite." I rather like that one. Well we could go on but we'd be here all day.... But as I scan ... moving down ... down ... nowhere do I find on the list one of the great pieces of political satire "A Modest Proposal."

(HARRY holds up the book.)

BRIAN. Maybe they forgot it.
HARRY. Let's hope not.

BRIAN. Or maybe they filed it under something else.

HARRY. Good point! Let's try looking under ... "Famine." Maybe I'm doing a paper about "The Politics of Hunger." So I type in "Famine".... No I'll even get more specific.... I'll type "Famine, Ireland." *(Types.)* And I get ... *(Reads:)* "1. Famine in Ulster, The Regional Impact, 2. Famine in Waterford 1845-1850, 3. Famine in Zimbabwe, 4. Famine in Bengal." Then a space and "Your entry Famine in Ireland would be here." Ah! So there's no such listing. I got close ... Famine in Ulster. But I'm not going to find "A Modest Proposal" here.

BRIAN. Why don't you just write in the title of the book and get it?

HARRY. I'm an undereducated student who has never heard of "A Modest Proposal." I don't know the title. I don't know it exists. I want the damn library to lead me to it so I can discover it! What the hell good is this machine if it can't help me? *(He gives it a swat and walks away, turns.)* When you walked into my father's store and said to him, "I need a tool to fix my thing-a-ma-jig, he'd say ... "Ah ... well ... try this ... and if this doesn't work try this in combination with this!" You are lost in repair your house hell and my dad rescues you. Today you go into a Home Depot, a store the size of a football field. First you search for a salesman in this abyss. Then ask him if he knows anything about "thing-a-ma-jigs." He says ... "No ... I sell telephones." So, you wander around in this discount jungle trying to find a man who hopefully can help you ... to find the tool to fix your house. If you do find another salesman, unlike my father in his overstuffed old store, he doesn't know who you are. Doesn't particularly care and doesn't know how to get what you need. It has never occurred to some dolt sitting in a windowless room somewhere in East Japip, copying cards into the data base that we need help! They leave it to US to do the work. They leave it to us to spend hours searching the data base for the books we need. Plodding through the jungle, hoping to come to the clearing. These old, clunky card catalogues do it for us! Zap! They are our Map! These computers are sending students out into the jungle without a map. This is the age of information age and we are less informed than a novice in a medieval monastery. We are undereducated and over entertained. This is progress? This is insanity!

(He points remote at bomb.)

BRIAN. NO! Don't! Look … I've got a family out there. You've got people … that … that … care for you.

HARRY. Name one.

BRIAN. Now look, this is not something you really want to do. I know you don't want to do it. I know the way you feel about this building. I don't know much but I know you don't want die for something if you can live for it.

HARRY. What do you care. You don't care.

BRIAN. Of course I care, what the hell do you think I'm doing in here? I don't tell my wife what I do anymore because she's scared some guy like you is gonna blow me to kingdom come. I don't wanna upset her. I lie to her. I tell her I had an easy day. And she feels good. She knows I was trying to talk some guy like you out of blowing us up, but she prefers the lie. So, I mean, if I didn't care about you I wouldn't put myself and my family through all this, right?

HARRY. I have no idea. I wouldn't do what you do for all the tea in China.

BRIAN. And I wouldn't do what you do.

HARRY. "And that said John … is that."

BRIAN. What?

HARRY. A.A. Milne. Your Mom didn't read you those poems when you were a child? "John had great big waterproof boots on/ John had a great big waterproof hat/ John had a great big waterproof Mackintosh/ And that said John is that."

BRIAN. Never heard it.

HARRY. You heard of Winnie the Pooh?

BRIAN. I think I heard of him.

HARRY. He was a bear. A toy bear who had a real life. He was hooked on honey. And not very bright. Surely your Mother read you ….

BRIAN. My mother didn't have time to read to me. She had eight kids! I had three brothers and four sisters. When it was time for bed you went to bed cause if you didn't my Dad would hit you with his belt.

HARRY. I'm sorry.

BRIAN. What are you sorry for. It was great. Just cause I didn't read books ... about bears doesn't mean it wasn't great!

HARRY. Okay.

BRIAN. It was great!

HARRY. Okay. It was great. Why'd you a cop. Why not a fisherman?

BRIAN. When you grew up where I did, you were either a priest or a cop. I knew I didn't wanna be a priest cause I'd already met Elena ...my wife and I wasn't about to give that up.

HARRY. You did that before you were married?

BRIAN. Sure. Then we went to confession. I knew I was gonna marry her anyway, so what the hell. If it weren't for confession, nobody'd be Catholic. *(Points to remote.)* Would you put that thing away?

HARRY. *(Ignores BRIAN's request.)* But why be a cop? Just because everyone else becomes a cop?

BRIAN. I wanted to be a cop. My uncle was a cop. My dad wanted to be a cop but drank too much. I mean not that cops didn't drink, but Dad knew he was no good when he was drunk. He drove a bus.

HARRY. That's consoling.

BRIAN. My uncle was terrific. And I wanted to be like him. And anyhow when I started out being a cop it was pretty safe. It was before drugs. Before the poor neighborhoods fell apart. My older brother, Charlie was a cop. A stray bullet hit him while he was helping up a drunk. Paralyzed his legs. My younger brother's a dentist. Not a particularly Catholic occupation, but he likes it. Now he has to wear rubber gloves cause of Aids. So we all have dangers. Two cops and a dentist. We play pinochle every Wednesday night. It turned out pretty good for us. Even Charlie. Considering. *(He takes out a pack of cigarettes.)* Do you smoke?

HARRY. No.

BRIAN. Nobody does. My desk sergeant. Me. My teenaged

daughters. Not my sons. I don't get that. I don't smoke much. I told my wife I quit. So I don't smoke at home. It's okay. I sneak out in the garage. Of course she knows. She can smell it. But she lets me. She knows I do it when I'm under pressure. Which is a lot. But I don't do it much. So she lets me. You mind if I smoke?

HARRY. Actually I do.

BRIAN. Fine. It's okay. *(Putting pack away.)* Would you put that thing away.

HARRY. Sure. *(He puts remote away.)* Have you tried hypnosis?

BRIAN. No.

HARRY. I tried it once.

BRIAN. For what?

HARRY. I wanted to be handsome.

BRIAN. Hypnosis can't make you handsome. *(HARRY just stares at him.)* Can it?

HARRY. I wanted to *feel* handsome. If I felt handsome it didn't matter what I looked like.

BRIAN. Did it work?

HARRY. What do you think?

BRIAN. I think you're — a decent looking guy.

HARRY. I don't care what you think!!

BRIAN. You asked me if you were handsome.

HARRY. I asked you if you thought hypnotism worked. I wouldn't ask you if I was handsome. I'm holding a detonator that can set off a bomb that could blow us to smithereens. So you're answer as to whether I am handsome or not would be highly suspect. If not totally worthless.

BRIAN. What ... are we talking about here?

HARRY. My hypnosis. Do you want to know if it worked?

BRIAN. Uh ... sure.

HARRY. It did. But *only* with the hypnotist. I thought she thought I was handsome.

BRIAN. Uh huh.

HARRY. It was a scam.

BRIAN. How?

HARRY. She knew I'd keep coming back to her because I felt

handsome to her. Even If I didn't to anybody else.

BRIAN. So, what happened?

HARRY. I tried to stop my sessions. But I couldn't. I was hypnotized.

BRIAN. Did you ever call the police about this?

HARRY. About what?

BRIAN. The scam?

HARRY. What the hell are the police going to do? Tell her to stop making me feel handsome. It's not a crime.

BRIAN. It's a kind of extortion. You were paying her to feel something only she could make you feel. She got you hooked on that feeling and you couldn't get off of it. She was your dope dealer.

HARRY. I was the dope. People can't give you things. You have to get them.

BRIAN. Listen, I tried to quit smoking. It's tough.

HARRY. Try hypnosis.

BRIAN. Thanks for the advice.

(BRIAN shakes his head, moves away tapping his cigarettes in his pocket.)

HARRY. You can go outside and smoke if you want.

BRIAN. No. It's okay. I really oughta stop.

(The walkie talkie squawks. HARRY reacts, moving to left of his desk.)

SENTANA. *(O.S.)* Dickey, are you all right?

BRIAN. *(On radiophone.)* Yes sir.

SENTANA. *(O.S.)* What the hell are you doing in there?

BRIAN. Negotiating. *(To HARRY.)* Sorry, I have to say that.

SENTANA. What does he want?

BRIAN. He doesn't want them to take away the card files.

SENTANA. Hell I know that. What does he really want?

BRIAN. That's what he really wants.

SENTANA. What the hell else does he want?

BRIAN. He doesn't want anything else.

(HARRY is moving stage right while he listens.)

SENTANA. Jesus Christ Brian, you've been in there over half an hour and you don't know a goddamn thing more than when you went in.
BRIAN. Yeah, but we're both alive and the library's still standing.
SENTANA. Get him the hell out of there. Traffic here is a mess.
BRIAN. I'll keep that in mind.
SENTANA. Let me talk to him.
BRIAN. *(Looking to HARRY, who shakes his head.)* I don't think that's a good idea.
SENTANA. I want to make him an offer.
BRIAN. *(Sotto voce.)* Sir, I don't think that's a good idea.
SENTANA. We haven't got all goddamn day.
BRIAN. Yes sir. I'll keep that in mind. *(Puts walkie talkie back in pocket.)* Chief's not happy. In case you couldn't tell. He wants this thing wrapped up before the six o'clock news.
HARRY. Of course. He has his priorities.

(HARRY crosses to his desk and sits.)

BRIAN. Sorry. The chief thinks I'm gonna come in here and say two magic words and you're gonna give it all up. Sometimes I think he has no idea. Couple of years back I had to go into this house where this guy is holding his two kids hostage. Wants his wife back. Chief thinks it's a piece of cake. He just tells the wife to go in and tell the guy she'll come back. Fine. So she goes in and they start fighting and she says no way that she's coming back. The kids are crying. He's gonna kill 'em all. It's an ugly mess. It was tough. It was hard.
HARRY. Is this hard or easy?
BRIAN. What?
HARRY. Is this a hard or easy negotiation?
BRIAN. This?
HARRY. Yes.
BRIAN. Well it depends on what you mean.
HARRY. It's not up to me to define. You're the cop.
BRIAN. Well, if you define hard as taking the most time, we

don't know. But that's not hard. Hard is …. Hard's when you've got a real crazy. Logic doesn't work. Your logic. You gotta get into his logic. And if you make a mistake, you could be dead, so it's like you're in a foreign country, with a maniac holding a gun to your head and you're trying to talk him out of it, but you don't speak his language.

HARRY. Easy?

BRIAN. Easy is the guy or lady who really wants to give up. Who's doin' it so I'll come in and recognize them. You know. You know that real quick. You can tell they just want somebody to listen and get 'em out of the mess they're in.

HARRY. Is that me?

BRIAN. Is that you?

HARRY. You're the expert. Am I the maniac or the guy in a mess?

BRIAN. I don't think you're a maniac.

HARRY. Would you tell me if I were?

BRIAN. Probably not.

HARRY. *(Stands to face BRIAN over the desk.)* I'm not the guy who wants out of this mess. I don't want out, I got into this because I'm a man with a mission.

BRIAN. Sure. I understand that.

HARRY. I am not a maniac.

BRIAN. No, I didn't say ….

HARRY. *(Paces along side his desk.)* I am a citizen with a worthy cause … no less so than Gandhi or King … or Samuel Adams … or … or Joan of Arc! My cause may seem small compared to theirs, but it is a worthy cause.

BRIAN. Yes.

HARRY. If my cause was unworthy, I would be a maniac.

BRIAN. Yes.

HARRY. If I was doing this to … to … make … soup illegal. I would be a maniac.

BRIAN. Yes.

HARRY. But this is a worthy cause.

BRIAN. Yes it is.

HARRY. How do you know, you don't use the library?
BRIAN. It seems like a worthy cause.

(HARRY crosses downstage of desk, then right of BRIAN.)

HARRY. I'm being ...difficult. Am I difficult?
BRIAN. No....
HARRY. Am I a hard or an easy?
BRIAN. What?
HARRY. Case!
BRIAN. Hard. You're pretty hard.
HARRY. You're just saying that.
BRIAN. You're pretty hard.
HARRY. I'm not crazy. I'm not a maniac. That makes it easier.
BRIAN. Yes.
HARRY. What makes it hard?
BRIAN. Jesus, I don't know. Can we talk about the problem? I don't really think this is important.
HARRY. I just want to know what makes it hard?
BRIAN. You're too goddamn smart for your own good. That's what makes it hard.
HARRY. I'm too smart.
BRIAN. You've got all these facts in your head, but they get in your way. You live in your head. I don't live in your head, so I don't know what's going on there.
HARRY. You're not just saying, "I'm hard" to flatter me?
BRIAN. Look, can we get on with this thing?
HARRY. You're not just saying that?
BRIAN. No. Look, what the hell do you want?
HARRY. That's easy. Send away the trucks. Get Stockerfield to sign an agreement. The cards stay. And you can all go home.
BRIAN. *(Thinks.)* Fine! Fine! I can do that.

(BRIAN starts out of the library.)

HARRY. Hold it. If Stockerfield signs an agreement, what guarantee do I have he'll honor it?

BRIAN. What do you think?

HARRY. None. Get him in here. I want to talk to him.

BRIAN. I don't think that's gonna get us anywhere.

HARRY. Get him in here!

BRIAN. Harry.

(HARRY points remote at BRIAN.)

HARRY. Get him in here.

BRIAN. Harry, you know Stockerfield better than I do. If he comes in here he's just gonna rant and rave. He thinks your nuts.

HARRY. I know more about library science in my little finger than he does in his whole overblown brain.

BRIAN. I'm sure of that.

HARRY. He's an administrator. He doesn't care about books. He cares about image.

BRIAN. Image.

HARRY. Yes! Librarians don't have a good image. He wants us to have a better image. We're thought of as ... you know ... wimpy intellectuals. He wants to bring in computers so we'll be thought of as more "macho." "Hi Tech." Image. It's the same problem the Jews had.

BRIAN. What?

HARRY. Image. They said, "They're old. They live in ghettos and wear weird clothes. They smell. Clean 'em out." Streamline our society with bright, blonde sleek young people.

(BRIAN walks back toward HARRY.)

BRIAN. Look, one of my son's married a Jewish girl, and I think she'd be offended by that. I mean we all know about the holocaust. We've seen movies. And my daughter-in-law's great Aunt and uncle were killed. You know. So ... it's not something you just throw out there to make a point. To scare people. Are you Jewish?

HARRY. Half. My mother. My father was an atheist. I'm half

Jewish half atheist.

BRIAN. Uh. huh. Which half do you practice?

HARRY. You don't have to practice atheism. It surfaces by itself.

BRIAN. Uh huh. But you know what I mean. Do you go to synagogue?

HARRY. No.

BRIAN. Uh huh.

HARRY. But that doesn't make me Jewish. Do you go to church?

BRIAN. Every so often.

HARRY. Why bother every so often?

BRIAN. Well, my wife likes me to go with her to the Christmas service. Easter. The big days. The Jews have those too. You go on those days? The big days?

HARRY. I go to celebrate my mother's Yartzeit.

BRIAN. Oh?

HARRY. To honor her death. Her life. I go for her.

BRIAN. As a Jew or as an atheist?

HARRY. As a son.

BRIAN. Uh huh. Why couldn't you just honor her at home? Why go to synagogue?

HARRY. Why not do it by computer? On the internet. WWW. Yartzeit.com. Because her life is embodied in the synagogue. In the building. *(He lifts his hands to the library.)* In the ritual. When I go there, I feel closer to her. If I could go back to the home I grew up in and walk into the kitchen and smell pot roast, I would do that. And be with her instantly. But I can't. So I go to synagogue.

(HARRY crosses left of his desk. Brian's radiophone squawks.)

SENTANA. *(O.S.)* Brian?

BRIAN. Yes sir.

SENTANA. *(O.S.)* We've got somebody here who wants to talk to Mr. Mendelssohn.

BRIAN. Sir?

SENTANA. *(O.S.)* We've got a close friend of Mr. Mendelssohn's here who wants to talk to him.

(HARRY moves closer to BRIAN.)

HARRY. I haven't got any close friends.
BRIAN. He says he doesn't have any close friends sir.
SENTANA. *(O.S.)* Get the damn phone to where he can hear it, we've got a person here who wants to talk to him.
BRIAN. He's got someone out there who wants to ....
HARRY. I heard him, but ....
MELINDA. *(O.S.)* Harry.... Harry.... Can he hear me?
HARRY. Oh Jesus. It's Melinda.
MELINDA. *(O.S.)* Harry? Can he hear me?
BRIAN. He can hear you lady.
MELINDA. *(O.S.)* Harry? It's Melinda.
HARRY. Oh Jesus, get her away from here.
MELINDA. *(O.S.)* Harry, what are you doing?
HARRY. Will you get her away from here?
BRIAN. She wants to talk to you.
HARRY. GET HER AWAY FROM HERE!
BRIAN. Who is she?
MELINDA. *(O.S.)* Harry can you hear me?
HARRY. She's the woman I was engaged to. Eighteen years ago.
MELINDA. *(O.S.)* He's not saying anything.
HARRY. She's the one who decided she didn't want to marry me. A week before the wedding. I helped get her through graduate school. I wrote her thesis for her. And the day after she handed her thesis in she jilted me. She used me. Why the hell would I want to talk to her?
MELINDA. *(O.S.)* Harry, I know you remember me.
HARRY. You're goddamn right I remember you! Go away!
BRIAN. Chief. Chief, I don't think this is a good idea.
MELINDA. *(O.S.)* Harry, I still think about you.
BRIAN. Chief, this is not a good idea.
HARRY. No I want to hear this.
MELINDA. *(O.S.)* Harry, I'm sorry about what happened with us.
HARRY. *(Aside.)* That was eighteen years ago. This is hysterical.

MELINDA. *(O.S.)* You're intelligent and interesting and ... funny.
HARRY. *(Aside.)* Notice she didn't say handsome.
MELINDA. *(O.S.)* And I don't want to see you hurt. Your are such a sweet sweet man, you shouldn't be doing something like this.

(HARRY grabs the radiophone)

HARRY. Melinda?
MELINDA. *(O.S.)* Harry.
HARRY. Melinda what are you doing here?
MELINDA. *(O.S.)* I'm trying to save your life.
HARRY. You nearly ruined my life.
MELINDA. *(O.S.)* That was a long time ago.
HARRY. I still remember it. Vividly.
MELINDA. *(O.S.)* I wasn't right for you. You know that.
HARRY. You were right for me up to the moment you handed in your thesis. The thesis that I wrote for you.
MELINDA. *(O.S.)* And it was a wonderful thesis Harry. And when I handed it in I had an epiphany.
HARRY. I'll bet you did.
MELINDA. *(O.S.)* I realized that I can't go through my life depending on you like that. I have to be my own woman.
HARRY. That's not an epiphany. That's a scam. You should meet my hypnotist.
MELINDA. *(O.S.)* What?
HARRY. I didn't force my help on you. You asked for it. I loved you. I gave it to you. That's what love is, helping someone who asks for it. I didn't do it to build your character. I did it to show you how much I loved you.
MELINDA. *(O.S.)* And I loved you for doing it.
HARRY. And then you left me.
MELINDA. *(O.S.)* Because ... because ... *(She is crying.)* Oh Harry, I'm sorry. I'm so terribly sorry. I still care for you. My husband didn't want me to come. He said it was dangerous. I didn't care. I have three children, Harry, and I still came. That's how much I care.

HARRY. Are you your own woman?
MELINDA. *(O.S.)* What?
HARRY. You left me so you could be your own woman?
MELINDA. *(O.S.)* Of course. I'm a wife. And mother. And a travel agent.
HARRY. A travel agent? Your thesis was on Victorian mores and their influence on American women novelists? You were going to become an expert on American women novelists. You were going to teach. You were going to write. It was a brilliant thesis.
MELINDA. *(O.S.)* Harry, you wrote the thesis. *(He sighs, nods.)* I love being a travel agent. If you ever want to go anywhere, please call me.

(HARRY is starting to cry. He fights to hide it, hold it back, but BRIAN sees this and grabs the phone.)

BRIAN. Uh.... Hello.... This is Detective Dickey. Lady, I want to thank you very much for coming over and ....
SENTANA. Does he want to come out and talk to her? Should we send her in?
BRIAN. Send her away for Christ sake!
SENTANA. What's the problem Brian?
BRIAN. *(Sotto voce.)* Leave me alone. *(Turns off radiophone, then to HARRY:)* Sorry. You okay?
HARRY. Me? Fine. It's just ....
BRIAN. No problem. The chief meant well.
HARRY. Sure. Tell him if he wants to bring someone over that I'd like to talk to ....
BRIAN. Yeah?
HARRY. My collie's name is Dennis.
BRIAN. Dennis?
HARRY. Right. He would bring me some comfort.
BRIAN. Well ....
HARRY. He's not worried about trying to be his "own dog."
BRIAN. OK.
HARRY. Shit.

(HARRY moves off in the corner by himself ... to cry. BRIAN stands, watches him. Turns to look at the bomb. Takes a deep breath. We should see that in this instant, when HARRY is most vulnerable, BRIAN is trying to decide if he should rush him. Grab him now. It should take an instant, but seems to take forever.
BRIAN starts to rush toward HARRY.
HARRY turns. BRIAN stops dead as in a child's game of "freeze.")

BRIAN. I was gonna rush you, but I didn't think it'd be fair.

HARRY. Fair? I'm going to blow this place up. You don't have to be fair.

BRIAN. I once grabbed a guy who was gonna blow up an office he'd been fired from. They took him away. They put him in jail. Ten years later he came back and blew up the building. I like to settle things. You know. Permanent. *(BRIAN stands awkwardly a moment, then:)* It's not like I don't entirely understand you. My wife has cookbooks. Old cookbooks. They're all over the damned kitchen. She's got this one cookbook filled with recipes passed down from her great grandmother to her grandmother to her mother to her. Scribbled on little bits of paper. Some in Italian from the old country. It's like a whole family history in that book. It's a history. Y'know. And it's personal. My wife says that when we got married she used a recipe out of this cookbook so sometimes when she goes back to that book for that recipe it makes her feel like she's a young bride again. *(They just look at each other.)* So I understand.... How about some coffee?

HARRY. Sure. *(HARRY moves to desk, reaches under and gets out his cup.)* I bought this cup in a market in Italy. In Colle di Val d'Elsa. I used to go there and shop and sip espresso and talk Italian to unshaven men in suits. *(Shows cup.)* I went there to recover from Melinda. This is my recovery cup.

BRIAN. Nice. *(He opens flask and pours splash in his cup.)* Want some of this.

HARRY. No thanks

BRIAN. This is my recovery cup. *(Sips.)* Cheers.

HARRY. It is good coffee. Good Italian coffee. I love Italians.

BRIAN. I love one of them.
HARRY. You ever been there?
BRIAN. Italy?
HARRY. Yes.
BRIAN. No.
HARRY. You should go. Before it looks like America. Before they clean up all the sweet little villages and build malls.
BRIAN. Ok, maybe someday I ....
HARRY. No. Go now! Before it disappears. Just like this ... this library will disappear.
BRIAN. Okay, maybe I ....
HARRY. It won't disappear like that. *(Snaps fingers.)* The slow death started with the administrators, like Stockerfield wanting to get rid of the files to "clean up the place." The files go eventually ... there'll be no library. Just a little store that's like a take out restaurant. There'll be stores on the street where you go and order a book. Like Chinese food. Like a burger. You wait, they give it to you. You go home. No grand vaulted ceilinged room to sit in. No long shiny tables to sit at. No echoing footsteps. No essence of place that gives books the holiness they should rightly have. It's just a Burger. You want it. You got it. Well ... that's if we're lucky enough to have even that. With the internet we won't have books at all. You'll just order a book up on your screen. Print it out or read it right there in the dark in the privacy of your smelly little office. After several generations we'll forget what it feels like to turn a page. To fall asleep with a book on our chest, to carry a book with you that you're hooked on wherever you go so you can read it between stops on the subway. The whole thrilling tactile experience of reading a book, pages designed by typesetting artists. Print picked by editors and authors. Dedications, prefaces and notes and even the color and size of the paper. Each decision making each book a mini work of art. This cannot be found on a screen. A screen is dead. A book is alive. In eighty years, four generations, no one will know the difference. *(He sits, remembering.)* I ... I once saw the original manuscript of Henry James' "Washington Square" in the rare book room at the New York Public Library. I trembled when I held it. I touched pages he had touched and felt his

energy. I saw his notes in the margins. I understand how he wrote it because of how he rewrote it. When I held that manuscript, I learned something about the man and the time and the art of writing and my own vulnerability to heroes. That will be gone. It will all be gone. These, them, those *(He indicates the books, the table, the library.)* will all be gone. *(He takes a deep breath to hold back his emotions.)* You want to live in that world?

BRIAN. I won't be around.

HARRY. Where no one will fish the upper reaches of the Liffey. Where no one will shop the market at Colle di Val d'Elsa.

BRIAN. I won't be around.

HARRY. Your grandkids'll be here. You want that for them?

BRIAN. Honestly, right now I'd like to ... you know ... find a way we can solve this thing.

HARRY. We can solve this problem instantly if you tell Stockerfield, tell your chief that I'm right. Harry Mendelssohn is right. The files are worth saving. Progress must be staved off at all costs. I'm standing with him. Take the trucks away.

BRIAN. I don't have that power.

HARRY. Take it!

BRIAN. It's not my job to agree with you.

HARRY. What is your job?

BRIAN. To keep the peace. Save lives.

HARRY. Anyone can do that! Agree with me and we'll change history.

BRIAN. I can't do that.

HARRY. You can't agree with me?

BRIAN. I can't change anything.

HARRY. Then what good are you? What's the point of coming in here if you have no authority?

BRIAN. I have plenty of authority . I just don't have the authority to save these goddamn files!

HARRY. Neither did I, before I made the bomb. The bomb gives me authority.

BRIAN. The bomb ... the bomb makes you dangerous. It does not give you authority.

HARRY. This is an inane discussion. I'm giving you a chance to make history and you're talking like a ordinary cop. Interested in law and order. Jesus Detective, there is more to heaven and earth than is dreamed of in your philosophy. You don't go fishing for order. You go because you can't control the experience. You married an Italian woman because she is not predictable. You and I are not all that different. We want some mystery in our lives. We want to keep discovering new things. We want to stand in a stream and wait all day if necessary for one beautiful trout. We don't want it sealed in foam and plastic. We want more. And to get it we have to seize the day, Detective. You say you understand me. If that's not a ploy, if you really understand me, then step over to my side ... and we'll stand together against the insidiousness of progress.

BRIAN. Mr. Mendelssohn. Harry. You're a likeable fellow.

HARRY. I don't really care.

BRIAN. Growing less likeable.

HARRY. Thank you.

BRIAN. I am a cop. I have people outside who are on my back. My job is to get you out of here with the building intact. My job is not to change history!!!!

HARRY. Neither is mine. But it has been thrust upon me.

BRIAN. Fine! It has not been thrust upon me. What has been thrust upon me Mr. Mendelssohn is the job of saving your life and the life of this library.

HARRY. This library is doomed!

BRIAN. Okay.

HARRY. Saving the building will in no way save the library.

BRIAN. Okay.

HARRY. If you want to save the library ... stand with me!

BRIAN. Okay. *(Into walkie talkie.)* Chief?

SENTANA. Yeah?

BRIAN. I'm coming out. I gotta talk to you.

SENTANA. Any progress.

BRIAN. I gotta talk.

(BRIAN turns it off, starts out.)

HARRY. Where are you going?
BRIAN. Talk to my chief.
HARRY. About what?
BRIAN. About …. *(He stops to calm himself down.)* This is not good for me. I'm not going to make it to retirement.

(He walks out quickly as HARRY yells after him.)

HARRY. Retire now. Join with me. We'll go to Italy together. You and me and your wife! I'd like to meet her. *(The door closes. HARRY's alone. A helicopter flies over. HARRY looks up. Then quickly moves to the phone. Puts the receiver back on. Dials.)* Hello. Jennifer. It's your brother. Why? Because we haven't talked in a while and .Jennifer don't get angry at me I haven't got much time. No, I never heard of that drug. Does it work? So what if it makes you drowsy if it relieves anxiety? Well if you prefer anxiety to drowsiness don't take the pills! That's the choice. I don't make the pills, I'm not giving you the choice, the drug manufacturer is giving you the choice! I did not call you to upset you, I called you to say good-bye! *(She hangs up.)* Hello? *(He sighs, redials.)* Jennifer what'd ya hang up for? I did not say good-bye, I said I called to say good-bye. Aren't you curious why I called to say good-bye? What? You met a guy. Great. A veterinarian. Great. You really like him. That's great. That's … he's married. Uhhhh Jen … no. Jen he's not going to leave his wife for you, you just met him. He's just saying that so he can get into your …. *(Shouts.)* What do you mean I don't know him. You just met him. You don't know him! Jennifer. Jen ... Jen …. *(He looks at the phone. Why has he called?)* Jennifer. I gotta go.

*(He hangs up quickly.
BRIAN enters.)*

BRIAN. Okay. I talked to the chief. I talked to Stockerfield. This is the deal. We are gonna give you a plane ticket. To Paris. To Italy. Whatever. You are gonna get a fully paid two week vacation. Either of those places. Both those places. We walk outta here … you go to

Italy ... that place you like ... and there's no hard feelings.

HARRY. And they take away the cards.

BRIAN. Look, the cards are gone. You blow this place up, they're gone. You go to Italy they're gone, but *you're alive and well and living in Italy.* You're a bright guy. Which sounds better? Gone and dead? Or gone and in Italy?

HARRY. Gone and dead. It makes a statement.

BRIAN. Fuck the statement Harry! In a week nobody will remember your damn statement. The world doesn't give a shit about library cards.

HARRY. Catalogue cards!!!

BRIAN. The world doesn't give a shit. They don't give a shit that I haven't had a raise in five years. They don't give a shit that the top executives in this country make zillions and zillions of dollars that they can't possibly spend while millions of people are sleeping in the street. They don't give a shit. Harry, save yourself. You walk outside, every TV station in town is gonna' interview you. You can make a statement. You blow this place up ... you're just gonna make a mess. *(HARRY doesn't react.)* How about it?

HARRY. You don't understand.

BRIAN. Yeah, ... yeah I think I do. *(BRIAN whips out a gun.)* Harry, I brought this back with me. I didn't wanna, but I did. So put your hands up, and come with me or I'm gonna have to blow your head off.

HARRY. Detective, I am so disappointed in you.

BRIAN. You and most of my kids.

HARRY. I thought I'd convinced you.

BRIAN. You got me thinking. That's true.

HARRY. I thought you understood.

BRIAN. I understand. The new system stinks. I buy that. I'm with you. Okay! Now go out there and tell the people with the microphones.

HARRY. That's not good enough.

BRIAN. Harry, I'm not negotiating now. I have a weapon. I have authority. I'm telling you what to do.

HARRY. Shoot me.

BRIAN. *(Moving toward him.)* Come on Harry, I don't want to do that.
HARRY. Shoot me, I'm not leaving.
BRIAN. Come on Harry.
HARRY. I'm not leaving.
BRIAN. Harry, It's been a long time since I fired a weapon at anyone. I can't promise you what I'd hit. I don't wanna hurt you. God knows I don't wanna kill you. I just want you and me to walk outta here together. I want you to get on a plane to Paris or Italy or wherever and I wanna go home have a nice dinner with my wife ... finish makin' the fly I'm makin'. Watch the news. Maybe I'll see you. Get in bed with my wife. And hopefully sleep through the night without havin' to get up to pee. *(He is right up in front of HARRY.)* What'd ya say?

(HARRY gets up ... and kneels down in front of BRIAN, and puts his head right to the muzzle of the gun.)

HARRY. I can't.

(BRIAN can't believe this. Shakes his head in disbelief. And for a second lowers his gun. HARRY wraps his arms around him and knocks him down.)

BRIAN. Jesus!!! *(They struggle over the gun. BRIAN is bigger, stronger, but he's had a few drinks ... and in the struggle he is tripped and rolls to the floor with HARRY on top of him. As they hit the floor the gun goes careening away. HARRY on top ... gets up ... and picks it up. BRIAN lies winded on the floor.)* Jesus.

HARRY. *(Holding the gun awkwardly.)* I am disappointed in you. I am very disappointed.
BRIAN. I'm disappointed in myself. Jesus! *(Sits up.)* I'm outta shape.
HARRY. You were going to shoot me. *(BRIAN gets up.)* I am terribly disappointed.

BRIAN. Oh fuck your disappointment! Get over it! Jesus. Get a life! You married? No! You have kids? No! You know what a real problem is? A real problem. It's not library cards. It's coming home after an all night negotiation with some lunatic holed up in a building. You're dead tired. You thought you were gonna die that day. You get home, the wife says she had cramps and your kid is sick and when you go into his room to give him a hug he throws up all over you. This is real life. This is the good life. You wanna know what's worth saving. A half descent marriage. Fuck library cards, they should stop throwing out marriage and maybe people would stay together. People who hated each other used to stay together for their children. My folks did that. Bless 'em. They kept their hate a secret and they stayed together. They knew what was worth saving. They saved my brothers and my sisters. And they saved me. Jesus. Save something worthwhile. Get married. And have kids. And make 'em read all these books and save the planet for Chrissake.

(HARRY pulls out the remote and points it.)

HARRY. I think you'd better leave now. You can't help me so I think you'd better leave. When you get out there, have everyone move away. I'll give you five minutes and then I'm going to blow this place up.
BRIAN. But you love this place.
HARRY. That's the point!
BRIAN. What's the point?
HARRY. I don't want to see it disintegrate slowly, year after year after year. I don't want to be here when they finally sell off the property so they can tear it down and turn it into another mall. There's a Burger King in London, at 30 Strand. Where Dickens worked in a blacking factory as a little boy. You think there'd at least be a bookstore. I don't want to be here when The Gap and Starbucks and Benneton and Eddie Bauer build their temples. I don't want to see this place boarded up for months and then vandalized and finally torn down by a gang of deconstruction workers who never read a book. I want to do it. I want to do it. I WANT TO DO IT!! *(Points the remote*

at him.) Go!

(BRIAN takes a deep breath and starts to walk toward him.)

    BRIAN. Give me that thing.

(As BRIAN moves toward him, HARRY retreats.)

    HARRY. There's no reason for you to die. Go!
    BRIAN. Give me that.

(HARRY points the remote straight out.)

    HARRY. I'll do it. I swear to God.
    BRIAN. OK. Do it.

(BRIAN lunges toward him; HARRY presses the button. Nothing happens. He retreats pressing the button as he goes.)

    HARRY. Shit. *(Press.)* Shit. *(Press.)* Shit! *(He rushes away from BRIAN, now keeping the desk between them as BRIAN rushes toward him. Press.)* No! Don't touch me. NO!

(He grabs the gun, points it at BRIAN.)

BRIAN. Come on. I don't wanna call in the guys from the street. They're gonna hurt you. Why not just walk out nice and calm with me?
    HARRY. No.
    BRIAN. Come on Harry. I wanna get home to my wife. She's probably heard this all on the news already and she's worried sick so ....
    HARRY. Call her.
    BRIAN. Harry, we haven't got time for this.
    HARRY. Call her. Tell her you're all right.
    BRIAN. But I'm not all right. You're pointing a gun at me.

HARRY. She doesn't know that. Call her.
BRIAN. Harry.
HARRY. Call her! I want to talk to her.

(BRIAN shakes his head. What to do? Sighs, moves to the phone. Dials.)

BRIAN. Hi. I'm at work. You did? Well I'm still here. Yeah, I'm with the guy. He's ... uh ... he's fine. He's okay. He's an interesting guy. No. I'm okay.
HARRY. I want to talk.
BRIAN. What?
HARRY. I want to talk to her.
BRIAN. Uh ... look ... uh ... honey ... this guy ... he wants to talk to you. I don't know why ... he just asked me to.... He can't hurt you on the phone, just talk to him. *(Holds out the phone.)* Here.
HARRY. *(Takes phone.)* Hello. Look, uh ... I'm sorry to cause you any distress. I guess maybe you're used to it by now but anyhow ... I've heard a lot about you and I just ... uh felt that I owed it to you to put your mind at ease. Everything's gonna be all right. Maybe not for me but for your husband. Okay? And uh ... listen, ... where is your family from? Your grandparents. Yes I know, where in Italy? Orvieto, ohhhhh I've been there. It's a charming town. I had coffee at a sweet café across from the church. You haven't? You must go! You have to know where you came from. You must go to Orvieto and your husband has to go to Ireland. It's ... it's ....The world is become homogenized. We have to hold on to our differences. Our cities all look alike now. You have to go before that little café disappears. Before it becomes a Starbucks. Before ... *(Holding back tears.)* You have to go. And he has to go. It's up to us, Elena. It's up to us to hold onto these things. The kids don't care, the kids don't know. It's up to us. Okay? ... Good. Good. Nice talking to you too. Good-bye. *(He hangs up.)* I like her voice. You're a lucky man. She has a calming voice. I'll bet she calms you down.
BRIAN. When she's not screaming at me. Yeah.
HARRY. Well she's Italian. You have to give her some slack.
BRIAN. This is not news to me.

HARRY. I think I'd have a hard time shooting you, knowing you have such a lovely wife.

BRIAN. Thank you.

HARRY. But I will, if you don't leave. Please. *(Points the gun.)* I want to get this over with. I'm going to set this thing off by hand. I can clip a wire. I know what to do.

BRIAN. Harry, it's over.

HARRY. GOOOOOOO!

(Points gun at BRIAN. BRIAN turns to go. Stops. Comes back and picks up his thermos. Looks for the cup. Moves to table to get cup and starts out. Stops.)

BRIAN. Wait a minute. I have a solution. I have a solution! You want to save the cards?

HARRY. We're not going to find ....

BRIAN. You want to save the cards correct?

HARRY. Yes, but ....

BRIAN. You're asking for too much!

HARRY. I ....

BRIAN. You're asking for too much. You're asking to save the cards and to keep them here. It's too much. Which is more important? Saving them or keeping them in the library?

HARRY. Both. They have to be saved and kept here so that ....

BRIAN. NO! It's too late to keep them here. The computers are here. It's too late. But if you can save the cards, then when they find out that the computers don't work as well, they can bring them back. They can bring them back because you have saved them!

HARRY. If they leave the library they'll never come back.

BRIAN. If you blow them up, they'll never come back. If you keep demanding they stay here, they'll never stay here. Your demands aren't realistic. You're not giving THEM ... the enemy any room to maneuver.

HARRY. I don't want to give them any room. I want them to ....

BRIAN. Jesus Harry, stop trying to be a fucking saint. Keep your eye on the ball. The most important thing to save is the cards. Yes or no?

HARRY. You can't just ...

BRIAN. Yes or no?

HARRY. Yes.

BRIAN. Good. I can get that for you. I can get them to give you the cards.

HARRY. Give me the cards? Where the hell am I going to keep the cards? I can barely keep a full-sized collie in my apartment.

BRIAN. That's a detail.

HARRY. No it's not! I don't want them in some warehouse somewhere. They'll rot. They'll decay. Or they'll sneak in and get rid of them when I'm not looking. I want them where I can see them. Touch them. Know they're alive.

BRIAN. We'll find a place.

HARRY. Where??????

BRIAN. I don't know ... does that really .... My garage.

HARRY. What?

BRIAN. My garage. There's plenty of room in my garage. I mean not right now. It's filled with all kinds of shit. But my wife's been wanting me to clean that stuff outta there for years. This is a good excuse. I'll clean out the shit. Take it to the dump and we'll move your files in there. All nice and neat.

HARRY. What good would it do me to have my cards in your garage?

BRIAN. They're safe! Nobody's gonna mess with them in a cop's garage. They're safe and you can come up and look at 'em any time you want.

HARRY. I don't even know where you live.

BRIAN. Just outside the city.... Look don't sweat the small stuff. ... I'm making you an offer here. This is a good offer. You can save the cards.

HARRY. And then what?

BRIAN. I told you. And then when the computers don't work.

HARRY. They may not realize that for years. Decades. Centuries.

BRIAN. I'll still have the cards.

DEFILED

HARRY. You'll be dead.

BRIAN. My kids'll take care of 'em.

HARRY. This is absurd. I don't even know you.

BRIAN. Hey ... don't you read history? Charles de Gaulle didn't know Winston Churchill.... I read this once. This is true. Charles De Gaulle ... the French general.

HARRY. I know who he is ...

BRIAN. Charles de Gaulle, got outta France when Hitler came in and he went to live with Winston Churchill in England. Didn't even know him.

HARRY. He didn't live with him.

BRIAN. He lived there. In his country. Same thing. And when the war was over, when we won the war, de Gaulle was ready to come back, when they needed him. Your cards will be ready.

HARRY. Your garage is England.

BRIAN. Sure.

HARRY. You're Irish. And your garage is England.

BRIAN. Don't get brainy with me now. Let's focus here. Okay? Is this a good deal? Huh? Is this a way out?

HARRY. I ... don't know.

BRIAN. It is. Let me make up your mind for you. It's a good deal.

HARRY. You sure this is all right with your wife? Maybe we should call her.

BRIAN. We don't have to call her. It's all right. She'll be overjoyed when I get all the shit outta the garage. I promise you. Very happy about it. Very.

HARRY. How do I know, you walk me out there and they grab me and arrest me and none of this ever happens.

BRIAN. You have my word.

HARRY. Your word.

BRIAN. My word is good. I live by my word. People in this city know, if I promise somethin', I deliver.

HARRY. By people you mean ... criminals.

BRIAN. My word is good! I'll shake on the deal.

HARRY. You'll shake.

BRIAN. On the deal. *(Holds out his hand.)* You walk out with me, the files ... the cards go to my place. Safe.

HARRY. And me.

BRIAN. I don't know. They'll probably arrest you. You cost the city a lot of money. They'll have to nail you for something, but there was no harm done. I'll make sure they don't put you away. It's no problem. I've got a nephew who's a lawyer. He'll take care of you.

HARRY. Is that legal?

BRIAN. It's more than legal. It's a deal. Shake. *(He moves to HARRY, who slowly, puts the gun aside and puts out his hand. They shake hands. And suddenly Harry grabs Brian and embraces him. And cries.)* It's gonna be all right kid. It's gonna be fine. You did the right thing. *(Takes him by the arm.)* Come on.

HARRY. Wait. I've got something for you.

(HARRY rushes to the stacks to get a book.)

BRIAN. *(Picks up radiophone. Speaks sotto voce.)* Chief! I got him. We're comin' out.

(HARRY rushes back and hands a book to BRIAN.)

HARRY. "The Hardy Boys Go West." Give it to your grandson. *(Reaches in pocket to get card.)* Oh ... and this is a catalogue card. *(Shows card from pocket.)* This is a library card. They are not the same thing. Okay?

BRIAN. Okay kid. Let's go. *(HARRY hesitates. He is staring at the catalogue card.)* Kid?

(BRIAN takes his arm and together, they walk to the door. As they walk we hear on the walkie talkie:)

SENTANA. *(O.S.)* Brian? You bringing him out?
BRIAN. Yes sir.

(They start walking out. BRIAN has SENTANA on the bullhorn.)

DEFILED 55

SENTANA. *(O.S.)* Good. Mr. Mendelssohn, please listen to this, this is very important. This is Chief Santana. I just want you to know what to expect when you come out here. There is a huge crowd. But they are under control. When you come out the door, you're gonna be hit by TV lights. Reporters shouting at you. Stay calm. I repeat, stay calm. No one's gonna hurt you. We're here to protect you.

(They are at the door.)

BRIAN. Ready kid?

(BRIAN opens the door, and suddenly HARRY shoves BRIAN out into the blinding TV lights and slams the door shut. And locks it.
HARRY rushes back in and opens his desk drawer and gets out screw driver. He gets a chair. Climbs to the dynamite on a column and starts to open wiring terminal on the dynamite. Outside we hear pounding on the door and BRIAN on the bullhorn.)

BRIAN. *(On bullhorn right after door closes.)* Harry! What are you doing? We had a deal! Harry don't do anything stupid. Harry. Please. We had a deal. Harry!

(Phone rings. HARRY looks. It rings again. He gets down, picks it up.)

HARRY. *(On phone.)* Hello. I'm sorry Detective. It ... it wouldn't have worked. You forgot about the new cards? The cards for the new books The catalogues have to be updated with all the new books or they'll be obsolete.... I can't update them. I was fired. I don't have access to all the new books! ..I can't work at another library, Stockerfield will blacklist me. No.... No ... it's no good. It's a compromise. Gandhi didn't compromise. Thomas Moore didn't compromise. Sam Adams and Joan of Arc didn't make deals. They saw it through. This is my cause. This is my mission and I am going to see it through. And someday, they will know I was right.

(Bang! A rifle shot rings out. Glass breaks in the library window.

HARRY falls as the phone drops. He struggles to get up.)

BRIAN. *(On bullhorn.)* Harry It's Brian. Are you all right? *(HARRY picks up the remote.)* Harry, are you all right? Harry don't do anything. Please! Harry. Please!

(HARRY points the remote at the bomb.)

HARRY. Oh God. Please. *(He presses button. Nothing.)* Please, if there is a God, please. Please! *(Presses. Nothing. Presses. Nothing.)* Shit. Shit. Shit. Shit. *(Presses again and again.)* Fuck technology!!!

(HARRY flings the remote across the room. It hits the wall. The bomb explodes!!
The lights go out as we hear the building crumble. And then the light from the fire comes up, lighting the scene and we see that the air is filled with cards. Thousands of catalogue cards floating. Falling like snow. Drifting in the air, filling it with a great, temporary, tribute to their own demise.
Music, "The Vivaldi Gloria" fills the air as the cards fall and ...

THE LIGHTS FADE DOWN ...

AND OUT.)

DEFILED

PROPERTY PLOT

FURNITURE

3 large wooden tables
11 wooden chairs without arms
1 wooden desk chair
1 rolling library cart
5 lamps on the upstage tables (2 each) and the desk (1)

HAND PROPS

Library bag with
    remote control (with removable back)
    pack with 9 volt battery (rigged to open easily)
    roll of duck tape

Hardy Boys book (Upstage left in shelves)
A Modest Proposal Book (offstage right in shelves)
Gun
Stage blood

PERSONAL PROPS

Money clip with library card, bills and credit card (Harry)
Glasses on lanyard (Harry)
Thermos (Brian's coat, right pocket)
Walkie Talkie (Brian's coat, left pocket)
Cigarettes (Brian's left shirt pocket)
Harry's Note (Brian's left pants pocket)
Flask (Brian's rear left pants pocket.)

ASSORTED BOOKS AND TABLE TOP DRESSING

On desk:
    phone
    memo pad
    2 pamphlet holders with pamphlets
    lamp (see above list)
    stack of 3 books
    large book
    encyclopedia
    blood pack (stored upstage of encyclopedia)
    rolodex
    pen stand
    rags (in US second drawer)
    mug (in US top drawer)
    screwdriver and wire cutters (in US bottom file drawer)
    knife (in US bottom file drawer)

Book (on chair at desk)

On DSR table:
    computer monitor (screen facing upstage)
    keyboard
    memo pad
    pencil jar with pencils and pens
    4 books
    4 chairs (on on SR end, 1 on USR end, I tilted on USL end, 1 DSR with end pushed into table)

On USL table:
    2 lamps
    computer monitor
    keyboard
4 books
3 chairs

DEFILED 59

On USR table:
    2 lamps
    4 chairs
    computer monitor
    3 books

File card drawers with cards for Jonathan Swift's "A Modest Proposal" and "Hardy Boys Go West"

Sample Library Card
(Actual size: 3" x 5")

```
JF
Dix      Dixon, Franklin W.
PB       The Hardy Boys Go West    / Franklin W. Dixon.
         -- NY : Pocket Books, 1989.
           158 pgs. ; PB. -- (The Hardy Boys #85)

#265, Sept. '99, $3.50, donation
         ISBN 0671674587


       1. Detective & mystery stories.
       2. Brothers - Fiction.   I. Title.
       II. Series.   ◯
                                      00 234162
```

DEFILED

COSTUME PLOT

Costumes for the Geffen Playhouse were designed by Tom McKinley

*HARRY
    Khaki pants with belt
    Brown shoes
    Blue bottom-down shirt, open at neck
    Navy jacket (not worn, but over the desk chair)

BRIAN
    Charcoal pants
    Black Shoes
    Mustard shirt
    Green barn jacket with accommodating pockets

*Stage blood was used when Harry gets shot at the end of the play. This was hidden in a small pack on the desk behind a book. Harry picked it up during the final phone call with Brian.

DEFILED 61

ABOUT THE SET DESIGN

The set designed by D. Martyn Bookwalter for the Geffen Playhouse production represents a library with fieldstone columns and walls and a marble floor. The circumstance of the Geffen allowed the use of the center aisle of the auditorium to represent the front door of the library. The card files were built as facing on the front of the apron of the stage, with two practical drawers, one house left and one house right. The offstage right door opened into the stacks. There was a large Grecian statue upstage center. Three tables with lamps and computer monitors dressed the stage, with their accompanying chairs. The desk downstage left was Harry's desk. There was also a rolling library cart, which played just stage left of the desk.

At the top of the show, the columns were bare. In the first blackout, the bombs (which were stored behind the columns) were wrapped around the columns so that when the lights came up, the bombs were obvious.

The stage left window was rigged with a breakaway pane of glass and a remote-operated arm as the shot at the end of the play came from offstage left. Concussion mortars were offstage right, and there were four confetti cannons in the front of the house which exploded at the end of the play, raining catalogue cards of all sizes on the front of the audience. There were also two snow roller baskets of cards directly over the apron of the stage, which continued the effect as the play ended.

This design may not work for your theatre. In that case, the entrance to the setting of the library was from the back of the theatre. Entrances to the library came down the center aisle of the theatre. And the card files were set under the front apron of the stage. This *is not necessary* for the play to work. You can put the entrance to the library on stage at any place that suits your theatre. For example: upstage right opposite the up left window ... or if your stage is large enough, anywhere on the far upstage wall (where bookcases are now indicated). The same for the card files. What is most important is that you get a feeling of the grandeur of the place. With the right furniture and creative lighting, solid walls might not be required so that even a small space can seem grand.

ALTERNATIVE ENDING

Pick up on page 55.

SENTANA. *(O.S.)* Good. Mr. Mendelssohn please listen to this, this is very important. This is Chief Santana. I just want you to know what to expect when you come out here. There is a huge crowd. But they are under control. When you come out the door, you're gonna be hit by TV lights. Reporters shouting at you. Stay calm. I repeat, stay calm. No one's gonna hurt you. We're here to protect you.

> *(BRIAN turns to Harry.)*

BRIAN. Ready kid?

> *(BRIAN takes HARRY by the arm and leads him out of the library. Up the aisle of the theatre toward the "library door." Halfway up the aisle, HARRY stops.)*

HARRY. Wait.

> *(He turns. Takes a deep breath and looks back at the library. Looks, looks and then.)*

Bye old friend.

> *(Turns back to Brian, nods...and they walk out... We can hear the library door open... The noise from the street, light...shouting...and then it closes. Silence. The stage is empty. The library there. And we hear a burst of music. "The Vivaldi Gloria." It rises...and fills the room...fills it with music that embodies the glory of this place. And then the lights fade...fade...down and out.)*

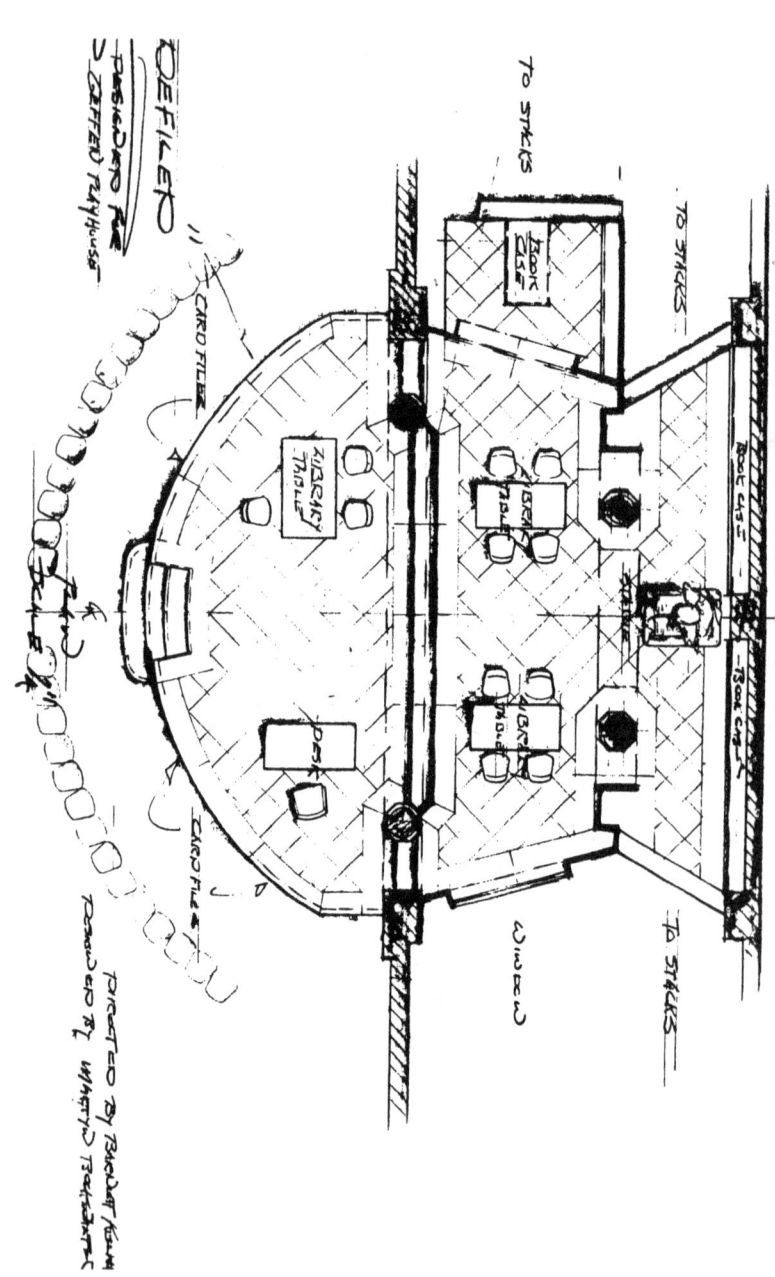

www.ingramcontent.com/pod-product-compliance
Lightning Source LLC
Chambersburg PA
CBHW051411290426
44108CB00015B/2247